IMAGES
of America

FEDERAL
HILL

Joseph Fuoco

First published 1996
Copyright © Joseph Fuoco, 1996

ISBN 0-7524-0288-9

Published by Arcadia Publishing,
an imprint of the Chalford Publishing Corporation
One Washington Center, Dover, New Hampshire 03820
Printed in Great Britain

Library of Congress Cataloging-in-Publication Data applied for

To director/writer Michael Corrente,
who through the artistry and truth
of his superb film *Federal Hill*,
has brought a renewed interest
to this most historic of immigrant settlements.

Contents

Introduction		7
1.	Coming to the Hill	9
2.	Christmas on the Hill	35
3.	Good Times	39
4.	Labor, Citizenship, and Activities	47
5.	The Church and His People	69
6.	Achievers	101
7.	A Settlement House	119
8.	Some Things Change; Others Don't	125
Acknowledgments		128

Introduction

Federal Hill is like a Steinbeck town. It is a quality of light, a color, a sense of motion, the smell of incense on a fall afternoon, the aromas of cooking day and night, a long main street, the avenue that begins at one end with a splendid arch and the hanging pine cone (La Pigna) that means welcome, and ends with a great church, its bell tower lit, marking the place.

Located in Providence, Rhode Island, one literally climbs to Federal Hill, for it sits, all 300 acres of it, high above the capital city. Over one hundred years ago, when the first great overwhelming wave of immigrants came from Europe, the Hill stood like a beacon. First from England, then Ireland, and later from Italy, immigrants arrived, settling on the Hill, building their tenements, making new lives for themselves, restricted only by language and custom. During the thirty-four-year period from 1898 to 1932, 54,973 Italians arrived at the port of Providence. Many were drawn to the Hill: in 1850 there were only 25 Italian immigrants in the entire state of Rhode Island, but by 1940, there were over 40,000 Italians on the Hill alone. From the waning days of the last century to the beginning of the new century, and even into the 1950s, when a third wave of immigrants arrived, Federal Hill has always drawn people to its heights. For Italian immigrants, the Hill was indeed the summit, the place closer to the sun, its graceful church steeples reminiscent of village campanile, the remembered place on the other side of the ocean.

Part nostalgia, part industry, part merchant and clothier, restaurateur and baker, artist and writer, the Hill is the true American melting pot. Great mansions built by wealthy English mill owners line the boulevard called Broadway. One street over, parallel to Broadway, is Atwells Avenue, the great avenue of shops, markets, churches and tenements, parks and plazas, crowned in its center with a superb fountain, a vision of the old world sitting majestically on a plaza in the new one. The bronze medallions set against the buildings and cemented in the sidewalks are carved with the names of the builders, settlers, and first citizens of the Hill; they tell where things stood, and where people worked.

The first simple churches could not contain their congregations, were razed, and were built anew. The great basilica and cathedral-like structures were monuments to an old world faith replanted, the faith of immigrants from Ireland, England, France, and Italy, especially southern Italy and the islands, places with magic names like music: Campobasso, Lucca, Caserta, Naples, and Palermo. The new arrivals brought their ways to the Hill, their adoration of the saints, processions, parades, feasts, and carnivals, their ways of cooking, of growing, of planting, and their constant desire to work, to make their lives better, to expand, and to be successful.

The era of the Pushcarts, on what was called Pushcart Row (now a memory), was an era teeming with life, so full, so overwhelmed with abbondanza (abundance), a world spinning with activity, noise, song, eternal music, colors, and families.

Battles were waged, some won, some lost. The Pushcart wars ended a way of life, of buying and selling; the successful moved from the Hill, and looked for stretches of prime land in the country, lands that resembled those they had left. Those that could afford it moved into the mansions of Broadway, just a breath away from bustling, bursting Atwells Avenue. Doctors, lawyers, music teachers, professors, merchants, dentists, inventors, importers, writers, singers, musicians of all kinds, judges, politicians, artisans, craftsmen, builders, architects, and orators, all took hold of the Boulevard and lived in great houses, moving from three-room tenements into twenty-room palazzos, bringing their treasures with them. This was success. Was this not what they came for?

Many did not leave, but walked the wide avenues and boulevards and the narrow streets all their lives, refusing to go. They would never go: this was home, this was where they had been forged, where their dreams had been given birth from their ideas, where they had merged, been brought into the bosom of a place called America, where children had been born and educated, where a new language had been learned, if not mastered, and where hope was always nourished.

Many of the houses are still here, the churches, the crowded back streets, with one dwelling wedged against the other, the cobbled streets, old walls with graffiti marks resonant and mysterious like ancient Roman fragments, the plaza evoking memories of times when raucous bands played for a week of festivals. The names of the streets are the same: Balbo, Europe, De Pasqualke, Africa, Ring, Acorn, Knight, names that evoke those who came first, and some who came later. Only a few have changed in the last one hundred years. Thus, when one speaks of Federal Hill, one is in touch with a special nostalgia, with images and stories of what once was, and will never be again.

The past of "Colletto" (or "Little Hill") continues today with its ghosts. Those that stayed and those that left are here in the walls, the houses, the churches; one hears their stories, their names, in the tenements and echoing rooms of the mansions; in the streets they buy their food fresh from the open and shaded pushcarts, laughing and arguing, debating and agreeing in their way; they can be heard in processions and in little groups on the piazza, and in the spray of the fountain, as it blows gently across their faces on a summer night. Music is playing. They have not gone. They still nourish the Hill, for all those who came, who climbed, who dreamed, who flourished, and who finally went to sleep, have left their souls here.

One
Coming to the Hill

The tenements of Federal Hill can be seen behind Mr. and Mrs. De Marco, new residents in the area. (Collection of Frank Ferri.)

A family sits for a formal portrait in a small Italian village, ready to sail for America. (Collection of Frank Ferri.)

From the poverty of a small village, posing for perhaps a last portrait, these people are coming to the Hill. (Collection of Frank Ferri.)

The *Augustus Genova* is bringing voyagers from Italy to the states: and to Federal Hill. (Collection of Frank Ferri.)

These proud, confident arrivals on the *Augustus* would soon call Federal Hill home. (Collection of Frank Ferri.)

Filomena De Marco married Gabriele Ferri on the Hill on February 20, 1922. A generation

continues. (Collection of Frank Ferri.).

More than a party, a real bash was held on the *Augustus* as it neared the port of Providence.

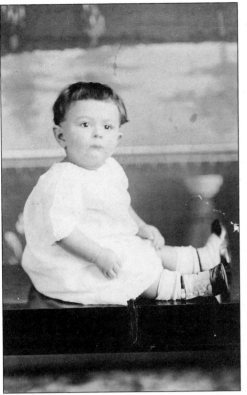

Frank, John, and Gabriele were the children of Filomena and Gabriele. Generations flourish on the Hill. (Collection of Frank Ferri.)

The De Robbio family was a typical Federal Hill family in 1906. From left to right are: son Ernest, mother Angelina, daughter Vincenzina (Jennie), father Carlo Albert, and son Antonio (Dan). This photograph was taken at the famous Beniamino Ansaldi studio in the heart of the Hill, on Atwells Avenue. (Collection of Angela O. Barletta.)

Hardly toughs, these young neighborhood men of Federal Hill were photographed in 1917. Dressed to the nines, the only one known is Ernest De Robbio (front row, center). (Collection of Angela O. Barletta.)

Posed elegantly and stoically in 1914, with a child sitting on a little "throne," are, from left to right, Maria De Robbio, Querino Della Grotta, and Jennie Della Grotta. (Collection of Angela O. Barletta.)

Babies, infants, strollers, and lovers of the camera: the second generation is born on the Hill. (Collection of Frank Ferri.)

The fifties were a thriving time for the Hill. Few had moved away and families were growing. This man holding his baby is obviously proud of where he lives. (Collection of Frank Ferri.)

Families growing on the Hill, ever enlarging. The 1920s and '30s were the decades of enormous growth. Here mothers hold their infant children. Notice the clothes on the clothesline and the fire escape. (Collection of Frank Ferri.)

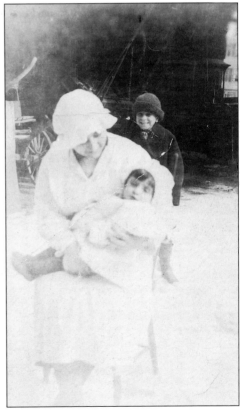

And who is this, looking like the proud owner of the ice cream truck behind her? (Collection of Frank Ferri.)

On the Avenue, a baby sits securely in a carriage. In the background is an ice cream parlor. (Collection of Frank Ferri.)

If you "build it" they will come—and here they are in their beloved gardens. Like followers of Bacchus, two devourers attack succulent grapes. (Collection of Frank Ferri.)

Looking proud as peacocks, a trio stands in their garden. (Collection of Frank Ferri.)

This elderly couple look as if they are being propped up. No, it's only an embrace. (Collection of Frank Ferri.)

Lovers, perhaps on a Sunday morning in the sun, are surrounded by grapevines. (Collection of Frank Ferri.)

Gardens fed more than bellies; they were also where families congregated. Here are three generations of the De Marco family. (Collection of Frank Ferri.)

Filomena De Marco (in the back) looks pleased and tanned with some neighborhood kids in a garden. The scene looks like a combination of *Tom Sawyer* and *The Arabian Nights*. (Collection of Frank Ferri.)

Filomena De Marco looks proud and pleased as punch over her sparkling white apron. (Collection of Frank Ferri.)

Alphonse Barletta gives little brother Antonio some moral support. (Collection of Angela O. Barletta.)

Here is Filomena De Marco on the sidewalk with her first typewriter. (Collection of Frank Ferri.)

A young woman of Federal Hill: neat, scrubbed, healthy, and happy. (Collection of Frank Ferri.)

A driver of a milk or ice cream truck takes a break to pose for the camera. (Collection of Frank Ferri.)

Little Frank Ferri looks dwarfed by shrubbery. (Collection of Frank Ferri.)

Broken, rude fences do not depress this gentleman, dressed in his Sunday best. (Collection of Frank Ferri.)

Definitely sweethearts, Filomena De Marco would eventually become Mrs. Gabriele Ferri. (Collection of Frank Ferri.)

Business is good, marriage is good, life is good: Gabriele Ferri is shown here near his delivery truck. (Collection of Frank Ferri.).

Gabriele and Filomena are shown here in front of their two ice cream trucks. Business was booming. (Collection of Frank Ferri.)

Gabriele Ferri, posed on the fender of his new car, sits ceremoniously near girlfriend Filomena's house. (Collection of Frank Ferri.)

If Gabriele can lean on the fender, why not Filomena? (Collection of Frank Ferri.)

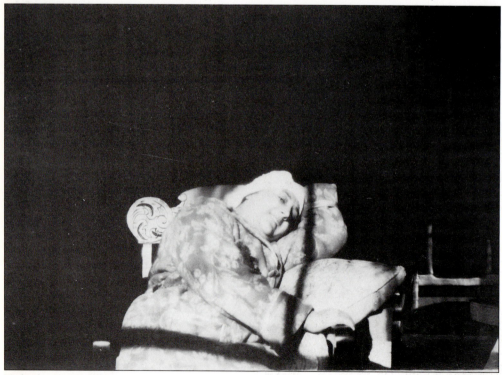
Nobody can say Filomena De Marco was camera shy. She seems born to it. (Collection of Frank Ferri.)

The old Paradise Cafe is gone but still revered. The car is a classic; so are the people. (Collection of Frank Ferri.).

There are no frowns among this bunch of friends on the Hill. (Collection of Frank Ferri.)

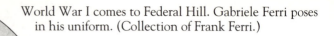

World War I comes to Federal Hill. Gabriele Ferri poses in his uniform. (Collection of Frank Ferri.)

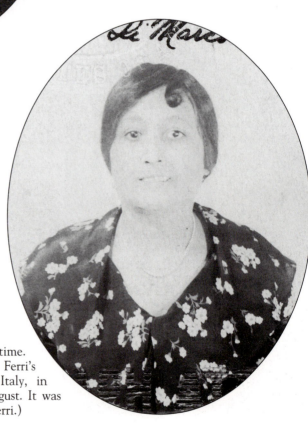

Everybody has to get away sometime. This is Filomena De Marco Ferri's passport. She went to Naples, Italy, in March 1931, and stayed until August. It was quite a trip. (Collection of Frank Ferri.)

Two patriots whip up sentiment standing with the flag in a Federal Hill studio. (Collection of Frank Ferri.)

This is none other than Joe De Giuglio, one of the legends of Federal Hill. He founded Joe's Acorn Market, which is still in operation under the ownership of his son, Joe Jr. Mr. De Giuglio represents the Italian immigrant who "made it" in the new world.

Two
Christmas on the Hill

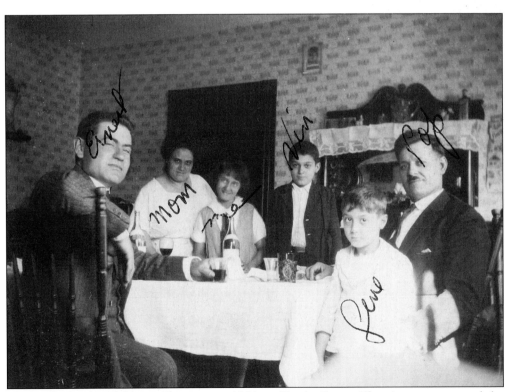

The Gallo family celebrates Christmas in 1924 on Knight Street. There's mom, pop, and the kids. Notice the telephone on the wall with its hanging phone book. The room is typical of the simple charm and intimacy of the Federal Hill tenements. (Collection of Antonette Marino.)

The Gallo family is shown here on Christmas Eve. The strong, stoic mother and father, along with their children and friends, some a little uncomfortable with the camera, photographed in a tidy room of the Gallo home. Note the essential bottle of wine, no doubt homemade, sitting as a centerpiece in the picture below. (Collection of Antonette Marino.)

When it's not Christmas it's summer. The Gallos sit on a Sunday morning after church. (Collection of Antonette Marino.)

Uncle Tony and Pop pose for a photographer one Sunday morning. (Collection of Antonette Marino.)

These are more scenes of Christmas Eve at the Gallos on Federal Hill. It seems like the room has become smaller with more relatives. Sailor suits for kids were popular in those days. (Collection of Antonette Marino.)

Three
Good Times

The Federal Hill baseball team, the first baseball team in the area, was photographed in the 1910s. Even the bats look different—and nobody made a million dollars a year. (Collection of Antonette Marino.)

Taking pictures on a Saturday afternoon was an exciting, elegant adventure. Notice the opulent fur virtually overwhelming the baby. The arcade was the place to go for such a portrait. (Collection of Frank Ferri.)

This is the face of an Umbrian angel, transported to Federal Hill. (Collection of Frank Ferri.)

Young marrieds, older marrieds: the faces are handsome and magnificent, if a bit serious. (Collection of Frank Ferri.)

This float was photographed on a downtown Providence street. The young women wear the traditional costumes of their Italian villages. Parades such as this continue to this day, and move from Federal Hill to downtown Providence and back, never really *leaving* the Hill. (Collection of Joe Fuoco.)

And a good time was had by all. These friends span three generations. The gentleman in the center, Mr. Thomas Marinio, lived to be precisely ninety-nine and a half years old. (Collection of Antonette Marino.)

This woman has the day off, and looks mighty happy because of it. (Collection of Frank Ferri.)

An orchestra stands in front of and on a veranda on Federal Hill. The origin of this event is lost,

but what a band it must have been, with that much brass! (Collection of Joe Fuoco.)

A parade and procession photographed on Pushcart Row, De Pasquale Avenue, in 1932. (Collection of Joseph. R. Muratore.)

Federal Hill had a picture theatre in the 1920s called Teatro La Sirena. Located on Atwells Avenue, it was the scene of much laughter and many tears over the years. (From *Working Lives*, courtesy of the Scott Malloy Collection.)

Four
Labor, Citizenship, and Activities

The pushcarts of Pushcart Row were teeming, alive, and noisy. Everything was fresh. Pushcart Row, more than anything else, defined Federal Hill. (Collection of Joseph R. Muratore.)

This is another view of Pushcart Row in 1938. This was one of the decades of the heyday of the pushcarts. Shaded against a summer sun, the pushcarts were everything to the people of the Hill, and everything they provided was fresh. If any image, any icon represents the Hill, it is the pushcart, the symbol of an old way forever gone. (Collection of Joseph R. Muratore.)

Selling bread, long and round, from a bread truck in the 1910s. (Collection of Joseph R. Muratore.)

A group of factory workers and students pose for a group picture in the early 1920s. (Collection of Joseph R. Muratore.)

The busy, busy tailor shop of Alfonso Baretta was located at 432 Atwells Avenue in the mid-1920s. Notice the metal ceiling and the well-used roll-top desk. (Collection of Angela O. Barletta.)

At one time milk was delivered by horse-drawn trucks. This is the Glicerio Perrino milk wagon. (Collection of Joseph R. Muratore.)

The men of Federal Hill were a very hard-working group.

The women worked hard as well. These women work in bright light from the many windows at Simonelli's factory in the early 1900s. (Collection of Vincent Simonelli.)

Everybody on Atwells Avenue knew John Marzilli, the barber. The shop, located in the Gasbarro Building, is shown here in 1925. (Collection of Evelyn Marzilli Sleszynski.)

The ice cream plant of Modern Ice Cream was on its way to becoming a legend when this photograph was taken. At this time, the plant was located on West Exchange Street, Federal Hill. It later moved to Balboa Avenue, where its legendary status was secured. Leaning on the amazing machine are brothers Tony "Slim" De Marco (left) and Frank De Marco (right). (Collection of Frank Ferri.)

In 1936 peppers were 10¢ a dozen and were sold by this vendor of Pushcart Row on De Pasquale Avenue. (Collection of Joseph R. Muratore.)

Modern Ice Cream became a legend on Balbo Avenue. Lines waited around the block for a cone. By now, frozen lemonade had been added to the menu, not to mention a 15¢ hamburger. (Collection of Frank Ferri.)

The De Marco grandparents, with grandchild, stand in front of Modern Ice Cream. People ordered cabinets then, in the 1930s. Farther north in Boston it was called a frappe. Not here. (Collection of Frank Ferri.)

Filomena De Marco Ferri poses delightfully against one of the sparklingly clean ice cream wagons of Modern Ice Cream. (Collection of Frank Ferri.)

By the looks of grandma a lot of cabinets have been sipped inside. (Collection of Frank Ferri.)

It looks as if the man on the right is offering some solace to the man on the left, who may just have to move that pile of metal. (Collection of Frank Ferri.)

This meat market and grocery was photographed on Federal Hill in the 1920s. Take a look at these items and exotic coffees (one of them sold for 37¢). The counter is so clean it looks like a mirror. This was during an era when even a counter clerk wore a bow tie. (Collection of Adolph Gianquitti.)

An oil painting depicting Sebastian Muratore Sr., around the year 1937, who for many years operated a fruit and vegetable stand at the famous square called De Pasquale. This painting was commissioned by his son, Joseph R. Muratore, who described his father possessing "qualities of gold." A plaque on the wall of a building marks the very place where Sebastian worked. (Photograph by Al Lothrop, courtesy of Joseph R. Muratore.)

On the Avenue fresh fish was the hallmark. In the 1950s this vendor sold fish on Atwell's Avenue, echoing those Hill ancestors who, pushcart to pushcart, kept the Hill replenished with gifts from the sea.

The Federal Hill House was a settlement house that offered myriad benefits and activities for the immigrants and the residents of the Hill for decades. It is still very much alive. The officers of Troop 99 of the Boy Scouts of America pose here at the Federal Hill House. From left to right are: William Mulligan, scout master Hugo "Zook" Zuccolo, Frank Collins (in the back), Anthony Perotta, and first assistant scout master Dick Young. (Collection of Hugo Zuccolo.)

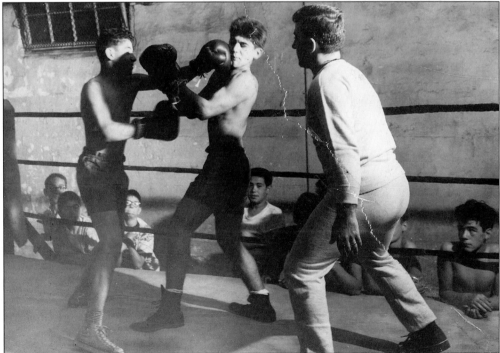

The Federal Hill House offered sports of every variety to the young of the Hill. Here "Zook" Zuccolo is teaching the art of boxing to Edward Brunetti (left) and Robert Pagnozzi (right). The year is 1952. (Collection of Hugo Zuccolo.)

A working family of Federal Hill over a half century ago, shown with a child of another generation. From left to right are: Elvezio Zuccolo, Angelo Zuccolo, Edith (Buoncevello) Zuccolo, Angelo Zuccolo Jr., and Maria (Fargnoli) Zuccolo. One of the eternal families of the Hill, the Zuccolos remain to this day entrepreneurs, residents, and symbols of the Hill. (Collection of Hugo Zuccolo.)

There was little more rewarding than becoming a citizen of the United States. Here a ninety-two-year-old immigrant is being sworn in as an American citizen by Judge Richard Licht, who later became governor of Rhode Island. The gentleman looking over the woman's shoulder in the center is Hugo Zuccolo, who made all the arrangements for the ceremony and who also taught English to those wanting to become American citizens. (Collection of Hugo Zuccolo.)

The well-known Gasbarro family of Federal Hill pose for a family portrait in 1914. Gasbarro's Liquor store, simply known for decades as Gasbarro's Liquors, was established in 1898. It adhered to the philosophy of "a good life, wine and beer" with a sprinkling of spirits. Gasbarro bottled wine and beers until the Prohibition Era ended such activities. During the so called "dry years," Gasbarro sold malt and hops as well as brewing pots and recipes. Its famous logo, a bunch of purple grapes, is known throughout the country. Shown here are, from left to right: (front row) Jenny, Edgidio, Ugo, Teresa, and Sozzio Gasbarro; (back row) Enrica, Francesco, and Antonio Gasbarro (the founder of the business). (Courtesy of Lombard Gasbarro.)

A good way to get any fighting spirit out of the streets was through boxing. This group, photographed fifty years ago, was trained at the Federal Hill House by boxing instructor Dante Sciarra (far left) and director Hugo Zuccolo (far right). The boys themselves are, from left to right: (front row) Edward Brunetti, Michael Martellini, Richard Tiberi, and Guy Tiberi; (back row) John Izzo, Frank Vecchio, Joseph Tiberi, and Richard Fusco. (Collection of Hugo Zuccolo.)

Gasbarro Liquors on Federal Hill was founded in 1898 and existed in this building until 1969, when a new store was built. Still located on Federal Hill, Gasbarro is now owned and managed by a third generation of the family, Lombard Gasbarro, wine expert and aficionado. Notice the letter "A" on the neon sign; it stands for Antonio, founder and maker of wine. (Courtesy of Lombard Gasbarro.)

This photograph offers some idea of the Federal Hill neighborhood, teeming and alive during one of its outside block dances on Tell Street. A very popular activity, especially among people who enjoy being together and who love a good time, summer nights were noisy and friendly. A thing of the past—this photograph dates from 1948—block dances were a common phenomena following the war years, during a time when America was at peace. (Collection of Hugo Zuccolo.)

This happy kid is probably talking on the phone with legend Joe DiMaggio. No kidding! In October 1949, little Peter Paolella had the great honor of meeting the Yankee Clipper as well as tennis star Pancho Gonzalez on the Joe DiMaggio Program in New York City at CBS studios (see p. 114). This was the result of one of the sports programs initiated at the Federal Hill House. Director Hugo Zuccolo is shown here with Peter. (Collection of Hugo Zuccolo.)

When Boy Scouts camp, they camp, no matter where it is. Here, on Federal Hill, smack in the middle of the Ring Street playground, the boys pitched their tents. The event, which took place in 1950, was called a Camp-O-Ree! And just about every Scout troop on Federal Hill participated. (Collection of Hugo Zuccolo.)

The Federal Hill House offered an amazing variety of activities to the youth of Federal Hill. A group of boys in a woodworking class of 1949 are shown here being instructed by teacher Salvatore Covais. Looking on is director Hugo Zuccolo, who was an integral part of Federal Hill for so many years he is known as the "Mayor of Federal Hill." (Collection of Hugo Zuccolo.)

The Uncas Manufacturing Company, the largest ring manufacturing plant in the world, was founded by Vincent Sorrentino in 1912. It ultimately became based in 1929 at 623–631 Atwells Avenue.

Workers also voted, and in 1932 it was clear the sentiments on Federal Hill were leaning toward FDR. And he did win! (Collection of Joe Fuoco.)

Working people who voted also learned how to save their money, and despite the prevailing belief that immigrants eschewed banks in favor of pillow cases or boxes under the bed, they indeed knew the value of interest and of saving a dollar. The Hospital Trust National Bank in Olneyville was one of the places Italian workers went. By 1929, many immigrants were well on their way to riches. (Collection of Joe Fuoco.)

Working meant also looking out of the window facing Balboa Avenue. Filomena De Marco Ferri can be seen inside Modern Ice Cream. (Collection of Frank Ferri.)

Some of the businesses and products of Federal Hill were very successful. As entrepreneurs sprouted, immigrants began to prosper on busy Knight Street. Raffaele De Angelis was one of the most successful with his Chemical Industrial Pharmacy.

The pineapple, hanging from an arch spanning Atwells Avenue, greets visitors ascending the Hill. It is the symbol of friendship—the welcoming symbol of Federal Hill. (Photograph by Kathy La Morte, from the collection of Joe Fuoco.)

Five
The Church and His People

This was quite a group. One of the great societies of the church, members, family, friends, and guests at an outing in 1933. (Collection of Michael Berarducci.)

The congregation of the Holy Ghost Church was photographed in the early 1930s. This portrait illustrates how vital the church was in the lives of immigrants who had moved from poverty to

success and become a force in the community.

The cornerstone of the magnificent stone Gothic church of St. Mary on Broadway was laid in 1864. It took four years to complete the imposing edifice.

Christmas Morn, an 1891 etching by Charles M. Springer, shows Broadway and St. Mary's Church.

This is the graduating Class of 1911 at St. Mary's Academy of the Presentation.

This could be members of a wedding, or more likely, young girls about to enter a procession in the 1920s. (Collection of Frank Ferri.)

Outings were big in the early years of the church. They may have been replaced by extravagant reunions, but in 1933 parishioners like these enjoyed a day in the country. The two priests are Fr. Bindo Binazzi (far left) and Fr. Parenti (far right). (Collection of Joe Fuoco.)

The Holy Ghost Church in the early 1910s closely resembled village churches in Italy. Renowned for its magnificent bell tower, the church is now completely restored. (Courtesy of the Holy Ghost Church.)

Three of the trustees of the Holy Ghost Church in the early years were, from left to right: Luigi Mancini, Tomaso Mancini, and Felice Nucciarone. (Courtesy of the Holy Ghost Church.)

These two photographs were taken on June 3, 1923, at the Feast of Corpus Christi. (Courtesy of the Holy Ghost Church.)

This is another image of the June 3, 1923 Feast of Corpus Christi. Processions were many and varied in those years, and the tenements emptied of people during the celebrations. (Courtesy of the Holy Ghost Church.)

This communion class in 1913 shows dramatically the sheer size of the congregation of the Holy Ghost Church. (Courtesy of the Holy Ghost Church.)

The Holy Ghost Church as it once looked: square, rock solid, and imposing. (Courtesy of the Holy Ghost Church.)

Now this was the way to go on an outing. This Holy Ghost Church outing in 1924 involved a float big enough to accommodate a small army. (Courtesy of the Holy Ghost Church.)

There were only twelve students in the first graduating class of the Holy Ghost School on June 22, 1926. It was a most serious group. (Courtesy of the Holy Ghost Church.)

It seems like everything was done in a big way then, even the annual church minstrel. This one occurred on April 1, 1927. There are some elements here that certainly would not be politically correct in these times. (Courtesy of the Holy Ghost Church.)

This could be a scene from Mascagni's *Cavaleria Rusticana*. On the Feast of Corpus Christi in June 1929, thousands face their church as the procession begins. (Courtesy of the Holy Ghost Church.)

Where did so many kids come from? On Christmas Day, 1929, between the great wars, there was a sense of security, of being together. Notice the pairing of the Italian and American flags. (Courtesy of the Holy Ghost Church.)

The Italian love of spectacle is very apparent in these altar decorations for a 1930s Feast of the Immaculate Conception at the Holy Ghost Church. (Courtesy of the Holy Ghost Church.)

This is very definitely a happy bunch of neighborhood boys, all Babe Ruth hopefuls, in 1930. Standing on the steps of the Holy Ghost Church with them is Father Joseph Invernizzi. (Courtesy of the Holy Ghost Church.)

81

Any church would be envious of these altar boys in 1931. (Courtesy of the Holy Ghost Church.)

In 1933, the Holy Name Society struck a pose with Fr. Bindo Binazzi. Again, numbers prove the connection between the church and its neighborhood. (Courtesy of the Holy Ghost Church.)

The graduating Class of 1939 was photographed on the 50th anniversary of the school. Contrast this class with that of 1926. (Courtesy of the Holy Ghost Church.)

There was nearly ninety in the group, count 'em. This was one of the largest, if not the largest, Children of Mary Societies in Rhode Island in 1939. (Courtesy of the Holy Ghost Church.)

The choir of the Holy Ghost Church is shown here in 1939. To the far right is organist Adele Gonnella, who remained organist for more than fifty years and lived well into her nineties. (Courtesy of the Holy Ghost Church.)

The intensity of a Corpus Christi procession in 1940 is reflected in the faces of its priests. From left to right are Fr. M. Albanesi, Fr. S. Zanon, and Fr. Ferronato. (Courtesy of the Holy Ghost Church.)

Black face was still politically correct when this kids minstrel show was photographed in 1945. (Courtesy of the Holy Ghost Church.)

In May 1945, five parishioners of the Holy Ghost Church were killed in a tragic fire. Their funeral, on May 7, is shown here. (Courtesy of the Holy Ghost Church.)

These Girl Scouts of the Holy Ghost Church were photographed in 1948.

This photograph shows the graduation of Violet Ann Zanella in the 1950s. The priests are, from left to right: Fr. E. Marino, Fr. H. Zanon, and Fr. J. Corrao. (Courtesy of the Holy Ghost Church.)

Here's another minstrel show, looking very politically correct, in the 1950s. (Courtesy of the Holy Ghost Church.)

The second grade of the Holy Ghost School is shown here waiting in line for some sweet Christmas cheer or to see Santa in the early 1950s. (Courtesy of the Holy Ghost Church.)

Women were integral to the church, and worked tirelessly to raise money. This is the installation of Mrs. Joseph Gattone and Mrs. Michele Corso in the Catholic Women's League in 1950. (Courtesy of the Holy Ghost Church.)

The Holy Ghost Church was home to seminarians in the 1950s. Shown here in 1953 are, from left to right: Alfred Almonte, Michael Tarro, Fr. Joseph Invernizzi, and Joseph Castaldi. (Courtesy of the Holy Ghost Church.)

Replenishing and planning for the future of the church; Fr. P. Bracchi baptizes a new parishioner in 1955. (Courtesy of the Holy Ghost Church.)

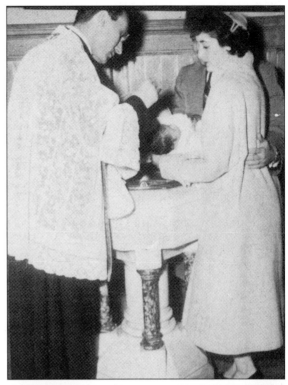

The interior of the Holy Ghost Church is shown here in 1953. (Courtesy of the Holy Ghost Church.)

Father Parenti's 50th year as priest was a golden time. Inside the church people attend the Mass; outside, the procession slowly moves within. (Courtesy of the Holy Ghost Church.)

This kindergarten class was photographed in 1957. (Courtesy of the Holy Ghost Church.)

In this moving photograph, Fr. Vincent Monaco blesses his parents after celebrating his first Mass on July 28, 1957. (Courtesy of the Holy Ghost Church.)

Father Alfred Almonte, a seminarian eight years before, leaves the Holy Ghost Church after saying his first Mass in 1961. (Courtesy of the Holy Ghost Church.)

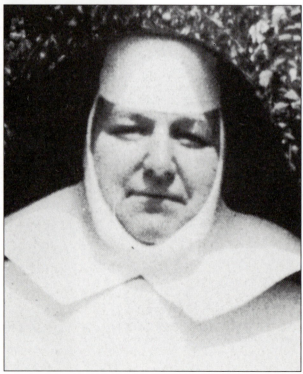

By 1953 the school had grown, and it was necessary to employ nuns. Sister Mary Paulinus, RSM, served as principal. The school was now fifty years old. (Courtesy of the Holy Ghost Church.)

The colorful, elaborate festival honoring Our Lady of Mt. Carmel is shown here in 1960. (Courtesy of the Holy Ghost Church.)

This orderly, attentive (at least for the camera) class of the Holy Ghost School was photographed in 1960. (Courtesy of the Holy Ghost Church.)

By 1960 processions had become much, much smaller. Some customs and traditions were undergoing changes. (Courtesy of the Holy Ghost Church.)

Mr. and Mrs. John Marzilli stand with great dignity on the stairs of the Holy Ghost Church in 1941. (Courtesy of Evelyn Marzilli Sleszynski.)

They don't make them like this anymore. A magnificent limo in 1941 awaits a bride, a groom, and a wedding party. (Courtesy of Evelyn Marzilli Sleszynski.)

Holy Ghost Church altar boys are shown here during a First Holy Communion procession. (Courtesy of Evelyn Marzilli Sleszynski.)

This Holy Ghost procession was photographed in May 1951. (Courtesy of Lori Ann Neri.)

Is he singing or yawning? Whichever, this 1951 photograph clearly shows that he has caught the eye of Fr. Joseph Invernezzi. From left to right are Vincent F. Neri, John Lancia (with his mouth open), Fr. Invernezzi, Henry Santopadre, and Frank Garafolo. (Courtesy of Lori Ann Neri.)

A day of days: the First Holy Communion of William Barletta took place at the Holy Ghost Church on May 24, 1953. (Courtesy of Angela O. Barletta.)

The full strength of the Holy Ghost Choir poses at an outing to the famed 400 Club on July 5, 1942. (Courtesy of Angela O. Barletta.)

William Barletta appears in these two photographs, this time marching in the May 24, 1953 procession that was part of the First Communion festivities. (Both courtesy of Angela O. Barletta.)

The sacred statue of St. Joseph leaves the Holy Ghost Church on a feast day, sometime in the late 1950s.

The statue was carried along Atwells Avenue by society men and the faithful.

This is the impressive interior of Saint Mary's Church on Broadway. In 1930, when this photograph was taken, the church was in need of many structural repairs. During the interior's extensive renovation, handsome oak hand-carved tracery was added throughout.

Six
Achievers

The immigrants entered here, at State Pier No. 1 in Providence, their own Ellis Island. Many who came were to become beacons and models of success in less than a decade. (Courtesy of the Aurora Club of Rhode Island.)

Antonio F. Cappelli built the first business block on the Hill in the early 1920s. His name still graces the old buildings of the block. (Courtesy of the Aurora Club of Rhode Island.)

Antonio F. Cappelli was an importer who achieved great success in the wholesale liquor business. (Courtesy of Italo Americans of Rhode Island.)

Oresto Di Saia was one of the most famous architects in Rhode Island. Born on Federal Street, he was largely self-taught. His designs included great churches, theatres, and fraternity houses. (Courtesy of Italo Americans of Rhode Island.)

John F. D'Errico was a successful broker and established a loan and brokerage agency at 119 Atwells Avenue in the 1910s. (Courtesy of Italo Americans of Rhode Island.)

Arriving on the Hill in 1883, the Batastini brothers became involved in the bakery business, and owned a large bakery on Delaine Street. This is Ottavio Batastini. (Courtesy of Italo Americans of Rhode Island.)

Pasquale Cesaro invented the Sunrex Oil Burner in 1927. He sold a wide range of oil burners, kitchen ranges, and rugs from his salesroom at 272 Atwells Avenue. (Courtesy of Italo Americans of Rhode Island.)

Thomas Russo, shown here in 1923, founded one of the largest paint and hardware stores in Rhode Island, located at 279–281 Atwells Avenue. (Courtesy of Italo Americans of Rhode Island.)

In 1927 Luigi Scialo introduced the popular Scialo pastries, confectioneries, and wedding cakes to the Hill. His business, located at 257 Atwells Avenue, made the name Scialo one of the most famous on the Hill. (Courtesy of Italo Americans of Rhode Island.)

Nicola Cappelli was one of the illustrious brothers who created the first business block on the Hill. (Courtesy of Italo Americans of Rhode Island.)

Ralph Di Meglio, shown here in 1914, was a pioneer in the true sense of the word. He was the owner of one of the largest grocery stores in the Federal Hill area. (Courtesy of Italo Americans of Rhode Island.)

This is a late 1890s photograph of Vincenzo Giusti, an importer and entrepreneur who was involved in the bakery and grocery business. Giusti specialized in high-grade products. (Courtesy of Italo Americans of Rhode Island.)

The success of Giambattista Monachetti offers more proof of the Italian love of food. Monachetti established a large wholesale grocery store on Atwells Avenue. (Courtesy of Italo Americans of Rhode Island.)

Joseph Castronovo, MD, was one of the early pioneers on Federal Hill. He was a surgeon. (Courtesy of Italo Americans of Rhode Island.)

Anthony Corvese, MD, was a founder of the Federal Hill House, the settlement house for immigrants and their children. He was a surgeon and gynecologist in the 1920s. (Courtesy of Italo Americans of Rhode Island.)

Luigi Maiello, MD, was famed for his art collection and gallery that he maintained in the old Barnaby Mansion on Broadway. Dr. Maiello was a descendent of a noble family of Naples. He brought his magnificent art collection to America, to his mansion on the Boulevard, from his ancestral palace. (Courtesy of Italo Americans of Rhode Island.)

Joseph Ferrucci, shown here in 1930, founded the Choice Macaroni Company. The company, which specialized in the manufacture of macaroni and spaghetti, was located at 280 Atwells Avenue. (Courtesy of Italo Americans of Rhode Island.)

Salvatore Chiappinelli was a pioneer in the jewelry business and a trustee of the Holy Ghost Church. (Courtesy of Italo Americans of Rhode Island.)

Michele D'Agnillo founded CALART, the California Artificial Flower Company, which is still in existence today. The venture began in a small, humble tenement on Spruce Street in the early 1920s and then moved to 32 Broadway. (Courtesy of Italo Americans of Rhode Island.)

Victor Sorrentino founded the Uncas Manufacturing Company, the largest ring manufactory in the world. He was a director of the Federal Hill House and in 1922 was a delegate to the Republican National Convention in Chicago. (Courtesy of Italo Americans of Rhode Island.)

A. Alfred Marcello was one of the first reporters of Italian background in Rhode Island. His father was a Democratic leader on Federal Hill. Mr. Marcello was a syndicated writer for King Features and wrote for *Variety*. (Courtesy of Italo Americans of Rhode Island.)

Ubaldo U.M. Pesaturo, shown here in 1905, was a Renaissance man of note. A writer, reporter, representative of the U.S. Chamber of Commerce, translator, and historian, Mr. Pesaturo was also a teacher at the Federal Hill evening school. (Courtesy of Italo Americans of Rhode Island.)

Luigi De Pasquale was a lawyer, jurist, and legislator. In the 1910s he was tremendously influential in the Italian community, and lived in one of the great houses on Broadway. (Courtesy of Italo Americans of Rhode Island.)

Antonio Capotosto, an influential immigrant who graduated from Harvard Law School, was an associate justice of Rhode Island's Superior Court. Mr. Capotosto lived at 61 Sutton Street, close to Broadway. He founded the Providence Grand Lodge of the Sons of Italy in 1915. (Courtesy of the Aurora Club of Rhode Island.)

Here is Paddy Read (right), finishing off a contender. One of the boxing legends of Federal Hill, and a member of the Federal Hill House, Paddy boxed himself to great achievement in the late 1950s. He KO'd this opponent in the third round of an eight-round bout. (Collection of Hugo Zuccolo.)

Here's a little achiever, young Peter Paolella who, under the auspices of the Federal Hill House, found himself in 1949 sitting between Joe DiMaggio, the Yankee Clipper, and Pancho Gonzalez, tennis-star immortal. The expression on Peter's face says "This is too good to be true." (Collection of Hugo Zuccolo.)

This is an interior view of the elegant Aurora Club, the place where prominent and successful Italians met and discussed business, politics, and life in general. They also ate magnificently here. The building was formerly the old Walton Mansion on Broadway. (Courtesy of the Aurora Club of Rhode Island.)

The famous and the illustrious came to the Aurora Club on Broadway. This is Rocky Marciano, the heavyweight champion of the world, who visited in the 1950s. Rocky Graziano was also a visitor. So was Tony Conigliaro, the baseball player. (Courtesy of the Aurora Club of Rhode Island.)

This group of Italian Americans, all members of the Aurora Club, are enjoying a New England clambake in 1953. (Courtesy of the Aurora Club of Rhode Island.)

Federico Curzio was the founder and editor of *Echo*, an Italian American journal that existed for one hundred years. He was referred to as Don Federico, for respect. When he founded *Echo*, there were no radios and no other local small publications serving the Italian community in the Federal Hill area. (Courtesy of Joseph R. Muratore.)

Dr. Antonio Fidanza was a famed, lovable doctor with a perpetual smile who delivered more babies among Italian Americans than can be calculated. (Courtesy of Joseph. R. Muratore.)

Leonardo Quaranto developed one of the largest clothing stores of his time on Federal Hill at the corner of America and Atwells Avenues. He also later became involved in the poultry business on Balbo Avenue. (Courtesy of Joseph R. Muratore.)

This magnificent, smiling face belongs to Francis Bassoa, a man who dedicated his life to healthful foods. The founder of Providence Cheese/Tavola Calda on Atwells Avenue, Mr. Basso was renowned for his use of old recipes, dating from a time when refrigeration was not widespread.

Seven
A Settlement House

Built in 1885, the Nickerson House served the community, and what was called the Italian Quarter. Children were fed, educated, and housed here during the day, and even in the evening, so that immigrant parents could work in the factories of Olneyville. The first kindergarten services in the area were offered here, five years before the public schools offered them. (Courtesy of the Nickerson House.)

The Nick, as it has always been called, is shown here in the late 1940s and early 1950s. By this time a new building had replaced the original 1885 structure. The Nick served the community in a variety of ways: as a nursery and day-care center; as the site of the first Golden Age Club, the first supervised playground in Providence, and the first health center; and as a summer camp for inner city children. (Courtesy of the Nickerson House.)

The Nickerson House Tigers posed for this photograph in 1929. The semi-pro football team was formed in 1925. (Courtesy of the Nickerson House.)

The Broadway Press on the boulevard of mansions sends a large group of neighborhood children to a summer camp. Everybody got in the act of raising money, including the now defunct *Echo*, the Federal Hill House, and even Tony's Lunch. (Collection of Joe Fuoco.)

More kids, twenty-five years later, sit like little angels, being entertained by a singer. Notice the little sign behind him: "Your Hit Parade" was a TV staple of the 1950s. (Courtesy of the Nickerson House.)

It is called the Senior Social Club, but this 1950s photograph shows some who seem a lot younger than "seniors." The trip was to Lincoln Woods, a vast recreation area. (Courtesy of the Nickerson House.)

The Nick was utterly destroyed by the devastating fire of 1959, but soon after a reconstruction program began. A new Nick emerged, bigger and definitely better. (Courtesy of the Nickerson House.)

"Everybody wants to get into the act," Jimmy Durante said. This proves it. Here are two outrageous types performing on Stunt Night at the Nick in the 1950s. (Courtesy of the Nickerson House.)

The Women's League of the Holy Ghost Church pose in a wild and strange variety of get-ups on Christmas Day in 1951. (Courtesy of Angela O. Barletta.)

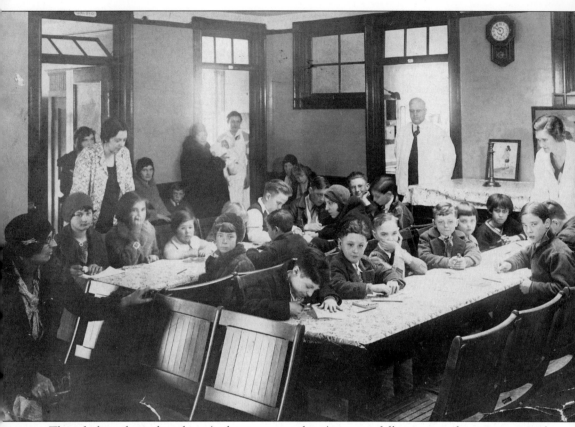

These kids are being kept busy (at least some are busy) in a carefully monitored activity room of the Nick in the 1920s. (Courtesy of the Nickerson House.)

Eight
Some Things Change; Others Don't

The Hill was and always will be a place where guys hang out, for no other reason than to be together, talking about boxing and whatever else pops up. (Courtesy of Antonette Marino.)

And older guys hang out, too. Casually and elegantly dressed, on chairs evenly matched, their arrangement looks choreographed. (Collection of Joe Fuoco.)

The Aurora Club was the premiere club for the successful on Broadway. Its exterior is a marvel of preservation. This building has not changed in one hundred years.

Going, going, gone! The magnificent church of St. John, so prominent on Atwells Avenue, was razed after it was deemed structurally unsafe. The church was a century old. Its superb frescoes, soaring arches, and impressive, proud bearing were destroyed forever. The site is now St. John's Park. (Courtesy of Albert J. Lothrop.)

Acknowledgments

This book would not have been possible without access to the collections graciously offered by many people. Thanks go to Frank Ferri (for the use of his vast collection of family photographs), Antonette Marino, Angela O. Barletta, Joseph R. Muratore, Hugo "Zook" Zuccolo, Lombard Gasbarro, the neighborhood churches, and the others who with a single photograph here and there added immeasurably to the entire collection. Thus, with the help of so many, we hope to have shone some light once again on these Federal Hill images of the past.